Little
Black Dress

Little Black Dress

Isabel Sánchez Hernández

A & C Black • London

Original title:
Little Black Dress

Original edition © 2011 **maomao** publications, S.L.
Via Laietana, 32 4th fl., of. 104
08003 Barcelona, Spain
Tel.: +34 93 268 80 88
Fax: +34 93 317 42 08
www.maomaopublications.com

Published in English in 2011
A&C Black Publishers Ltd, an imprint of Bloomsbury Publishing Ltd
36 Soho Square,
London W1D 3QY, UK
enquires@ acblack.com
www.acblack.com
Edited and distributed by Bloomsbury Publishing Ltd

Publisher: Paco Asensio
Editor, texts & illustrations: Isabel Sánchez Hernández
Texts: Macarena San Martín
Editorial Coordinator: Anja Llorella Oriol
Copyeditor: Julian Beecroft
English Translation: Cillero & de Motta
Art Director: Emma Termes Parera
Layout: Maira Purman
Cover Design: James Watson

Dresses: Isabel Sánchez Hernández
Dress on pages 66 to 75: Leyre Valiente
Dresses on pages 94 to 99 and 128 to 137: Miguel Madriz
Photos: Carlos Bandrés
Location: Istituto Europeo di Design (Palacio de Altamira, Madrid)

ISBN 978-1-408-12989-0

Printed in Spain

Introduction

This book is aimed at all those readers who love fashion, those with a passion for dresses and who are curious about the process of turning an idea into a garment.

This book is unique insofar as all featured garments are short, black dresses. Why? Because out of the countless aesthetic designs and styles on the market, we decided to pay homage to the *petite robe noire* first devised by Chanel, which in English we call the 'little black dress'. On account of its versatility, it is a staple in the wardrobe of all women. It can be worn to a cocktail party, to the office or out shopping, simply by adding a few accessories suitable for the occasion. It is a dress that allows each woman to adapt it to her own style so that, even where there are two similar dresses, they will never be fully identical because each will make it her own.

The history of this dress begins in 1926, with the great Coco Chanel, since when almost all designers have had a go at reinventing it. One of the most memorable and iconic examples is the dress created by Givenchy in 1961 for Audrey Hepburn in the movie *Breakfast at Tiffany's.*

Over the years, the little black dress has evolved according to the prevailing trend – for example, in the nineties, the decade of minimalism, focus returned to the original design. But while its shape has been adapted – becoming more or less tight-fitting or adopting a higher or lower neckline – it has always maintained its classic length, simplicity and elegance. The little black dress is a dress that still represents, like no other, the impeccable easy elegance of our throwaway age – the concept that gave rise to the original dress – and deserves its place in the firmament of fashion.

Materializing ideas

The garment, in this case the dress, is an idea that, once made, will occupy a volume in the space. There are several fashion-design techniques for constructing such a volume:

– The modelling method that directly creates the design on the body, without templates or moulds, simply adjusting the fabric to the body;
– The geometric pattern, the most primitive and universal technique that man has invented to solve the issue of clothing, which consists in the adjustment and manipulation of geometric shapes to find the design that is sought;
– The conventional or Western pattern, in which a pattern that replicates the measurements of the body is adjusted and transformed to obtain the desired shape.

This book focuses on geometric and conventional patterns, both separately and combined in perfect synergy.

In each example, there are step-by-step instructions on how to create the pattern for the dress along with the main indications for its assembly (though sewing instructions are not included; I recommend that you refer to specialist literature for these). The designs can be developed from any standard pattern – there are many systems for creating them – and for those who have not yet created their own pattern the examples used are included at the end of the book.

Finally, all the patterns in the book are a UK size 12. If you want to adapt a model to another size, because of the system that has been used to create the patterns I recommend that the pattern is constructed as shown and then the measurements are modified using any of the existing systems.

Semicircle:
Trapezoid dress

This design has a mix of concave and convex in its shape. With a very high neckline, it sits lightly on the shoulders and then floats down over the body. The last piece of the dress is of minimal volume for the purposes of comfort and ease of movement, and is the feature that gives this dress its own particular style.

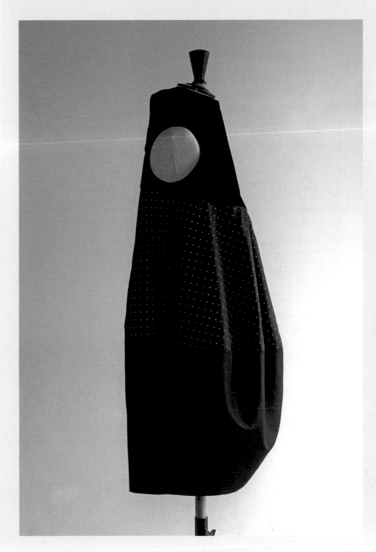

Each of the dress's three pieces has been made from a different fabric, and as such, it is very important that all three should have the same weight and texture so that the garment looks and feels balanced.

6. The semicircles are sewn in order, starting with the one with the armholes, which is obviously the top part of the dress. Once this has been correctly assembled on the mannequin and closed up, you can begin to attach the second one, and so on.

Side view of the three semicircles once assembled.

Circle:
Halterneck dress

This type of neckline, high at the front and tied behind the neck, is popular on evening dresses and swimwear, and stands out because it is one of the few garments that focuses all the attention on the wearer's back. In this case, the dress is made using just a single seam.

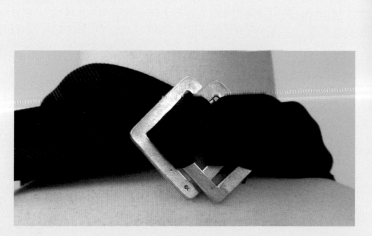

In this case, silver diamond-shaped clasps have been used to close up the neckline. The elements and materials you decide to use will depend on the style you want to give the dress.

5. To assemble the dress, the pattern is placed on the mannequin open at the front. The back should be checked, as shown in the photograph, to ensure that point B coincides with the centre back, more or less at the height of the waist, and fixed in place.

6. The front of the dress should be sewn by joining lines F–J and H–I together, working down from points F and H. This will be the only seam required to assemble the dress, and therefore the concealed zip should be inserted at this point.

7. The low neckline is shaped by crossing one front part over the other. Both parts should then be joined together at the back of the neck by means of clasps, which are used to close the dress.

Circle:
Cocoon-shaped dress

The shape of this dress is thus named as it wraps around the body at the top and becomes looser further down, just like the shell of the silkworm. It is made up solely of two circles, the inner one being the dress itself and the outer one being more like a coat.

Since two different fabrics are used – black for the dress, print fabric inside – I recommend having enough black in the latter to preserve the sobriety required of a cocktail dress. Here, I have opted for black and white, a timeless mix with a touch of elegance.

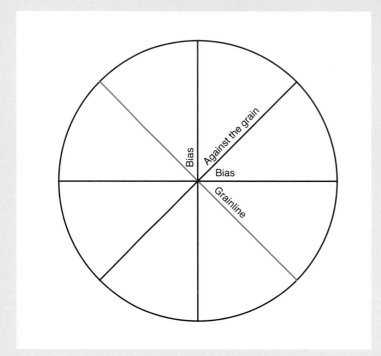

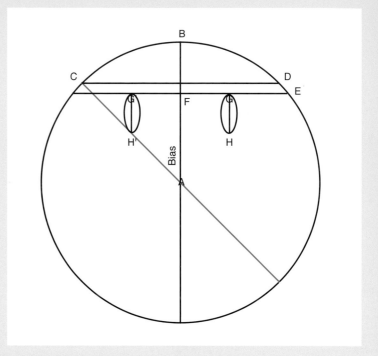

1. This dress is made up of two parts – one for the dress inside and the other for the outside. This is the pattern for the inside of the garment. To begin with, draw a circle with a radius of 60 cm (23 5/8 in).

2. Points C and D are drawn to form an 86 cm (33 7/8 in) horizontal line perpendicular to the line running from A to B. Point E is marked along this line 6 cm (2 3/8 in) from point D, and a line is drawn parallel to the one drawn beforehand. From point F, measure 21 cm (8 1/4 in) on each side to obtain points G' and G. At a right angle to these points, measure 17 cm (6 3/4 in) and mark points H' and H. Draw in the armholes between G' and H' and between G and H. Then cut out the pattern along the line marked C–D.

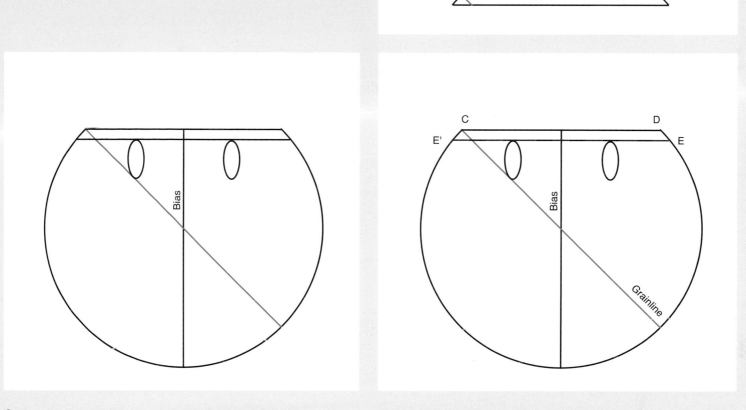

3. Cut out this pattern piece once in the black fabric and once in the black fabric with the white polka dot print.

4. To make the contrast collar for this pattern, cut along E'–E and mark once on the interfacing.

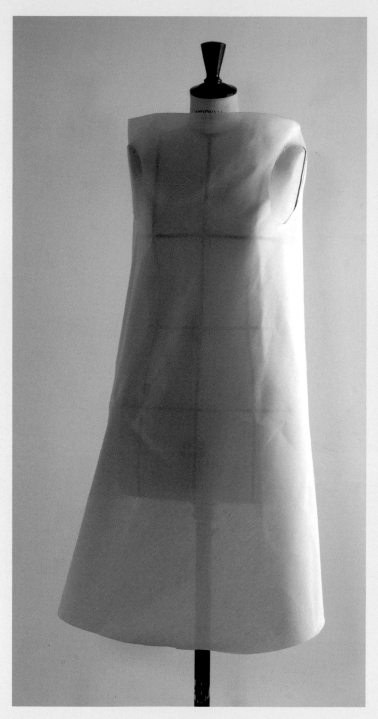

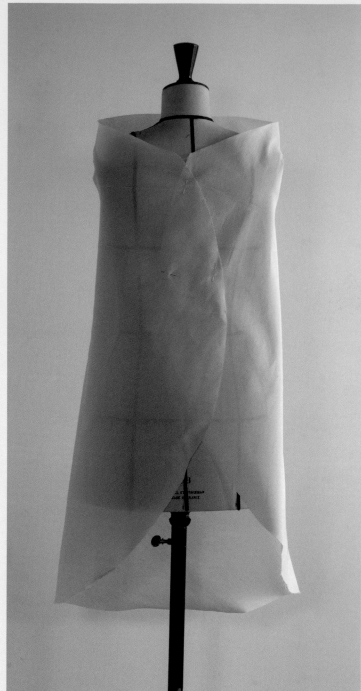

9. To assemble the dress on the mannequin, place the first pattern piece in position, open at the back.

10. To close this piece, cross the fabric over on the back, adjust to fit the measurement for the size being made up (in this case, UK size 12), then add the buttons.

11. Next place the second circle on the mannequin. This time it should be done with the open edges facing the front and lining up the armholes with those of the other pattern piece.

12. At the nape of the neck, turn over the pattern piece to form a generous collar falling almost as far as the shoulders.

13. Cross the piece over at the front and, at the height of the bust, make the buttonholes for fastening the ties. Having just one closure will give it a slightly flared or A-line shape.

Square:
Flexible dress

This halterneck dress has a hook in the hem at the front, enabling it to be worn two different ways: worn with its natural length, it is an evening dress; or, if hitched up to the loop at the back of the garment, it can be draped over one of the hips, assuming the length of a cocktail dress.

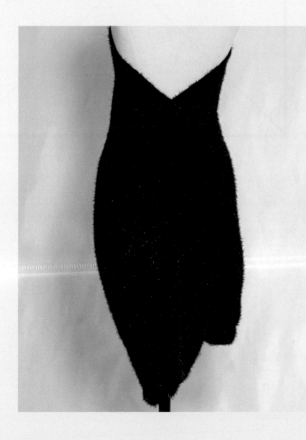

The dress offers not only these two possibilities – a long and a short version – but when shortened can also be hitched up on either the right or the left depending on how it is accessorised.

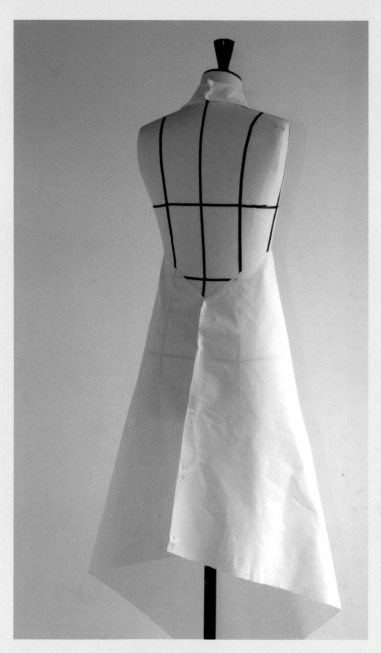

9. The entire length of the seam on the centre back is sewn up to completely close the skirt of the dress.

10. Adjust the neckline so that it fits correctly and measure where to put the loop or hook that will allow the top part of the dress to open or close.

11. Take the triangle of fabric forming the front central piece of the skirt and bring it up to one side of the low-cut back.

12. In order to gather and then drape the volume of fabric you have just created, depending on the occasion for which the dress is to be worn, place a hook at the angle of the centre front and a small cotton loop at the lowest point of the low-cut back.

Square and rectangle: Dress with draping scarves

This design has a fitted bodice at the front thanks to the dart in the centre of the bust. The volume of the skirt at the height of the hips has been shaped in such a way that the dress seems to have two enormous pockets, while the back looks like a long draping scarf.

The special character of this dress lies in combining different styles at the front and back. While the front plays with geometric lines, the back gambles on a loose and unpredictable drape.

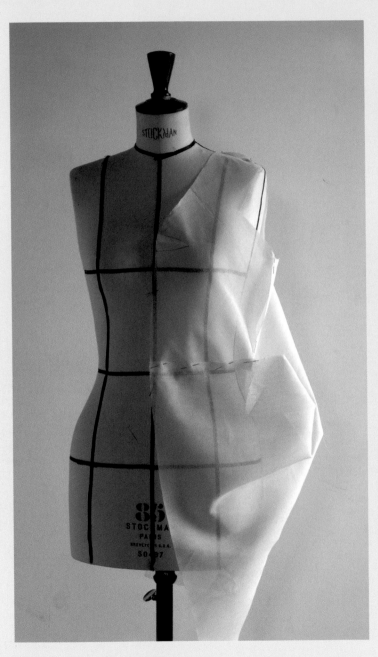

7. Now it is time to adjust the volume of the skirt. To do this, take up the excess cloth from the opening that has resulted from joining m to o (and m′ to o′ on the other side) and then gradually fold over to the inside of the dress, as shown in the picture.

8. The final shape of the dress is as seen in the photograph: the folds simulate enormous pockets.

9. Once you have the desired shape for the dress, it is time to close the dart on the bust.

10. When sewing, it is important to keep in mind its oval shape.

Rectangle: Wraparound dress

This dress has a beach-wrap style, a cut that is generally used for informal dresses, but which in this case has been made up from a fabric with sequins so that it can function as an evening dress. It is tied at the neck with delicate strings and has a very low-cut back.

You can add ceramic balls or beads to the end of the ties on this dress, in keeping with the chosen fabric, to give them weight. In this case, I have chosen some semitransparent stones to match the sheen on the dress.

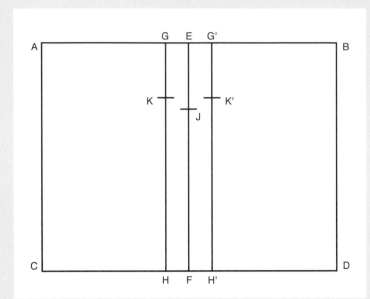

1. Draw rectangle A-B-D-C measuring 130 × 100 cm (50 1/8 × 39 3/8 in) and trace line E–F, dividing it in half. From point E measure 10 cm (4 in) to the right and 10 cm (4 in) to the left, and mark points G' and G respectively. Draw two lines from these new points in parallel to line E–F to obtain points H' and H on the opposite side. Then 29 cm (11 3/8 in) down from E along the line E–F, mark point J and make a buttonhole. Do the same at points K and K' on the adjacent lines, each one being 24 cm (9 1/2 in) from G and G' respectively. This pattern is cut once in the sequinned material.

2. To assemble the dress, place the pattern on the mannequin, matching E–F with the centre back, and crossing over the centre as shown in the diagram.

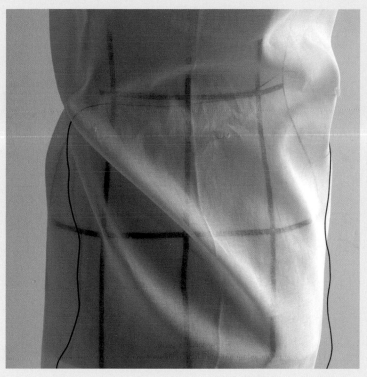

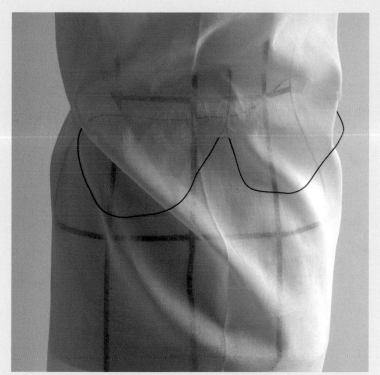

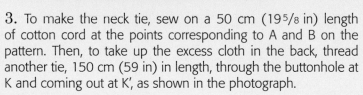

3. To make the neck tie, sew on a 50 cm (19⅝ in) length of cotton cord at the points corresponding to A and B on the pattern. Then, to take up the excess cloth in the back, thread another tie, 150 cm (59 in) in length, through the buttonhole at K and coming out at K', as shown in the photograph.

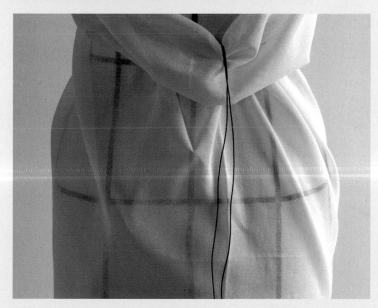

4. Then thread both ends of the tie through J and gather up the material. Once this has been done, put a knot in both ends. If you like, a bead can be added.

53

Rectangle: Dress with Japanese sleeves and lace

The bodice of this dress is reminiscent of the formal silhouette of a kimono, the typical Japanese costume characterized by its long, loose and very wide sleeves. The difference is that those tunics are open, their fit adjusted by means of a wide sash, whereas in this case the dress is closed and has a zip.

7. Place the p
close, and sew
neckline tightly
whether the ga
a ruffled effect

Lace, created in the 16th century and a feature of clothing styles ever since without ever really going out of fashion, is a very delicate fabric. Sewing machines have a special foot for sewing lace, which needs to be done with a 1.5 to 3 mm ($1/16$ to $1/8$ in) stitch.

Grainline

4. For the cuffs,
(19¾ × 3 ½ in),

6. For the nec
(98 ½ × 8 ⁵/₈

Rectangle: Scarf dress

This is a dress cut on the bias which starts off as a form-fitting garment on the shoulders and bust, and gradually flares out lower down. The dress has a lot of swirl in it, and given the cut of its neckline, the shape of the armholes and the different lengths of the hem, it seems surprising that everything arises from just a single rectangular piece of material with a hole in it.

This dress demonstrates that the complexity of a dress pattern does not correspond directly to the end result, and that, given careful placement of the seams, the volumes of fabric in the final shape can be really interesting.

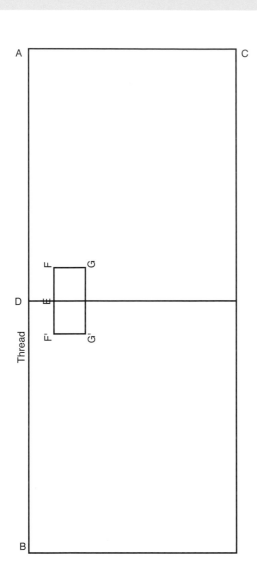

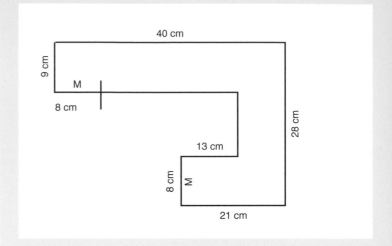

2. This pattern corresponds to the facing for the dress. Following the measurements in the diagram as you make it, bear in mind that all the angles are right angles, and the pieces should be cut twice in the chosen fabric and twice in the interfacing. Before going on to assemble the pattern, I recommend double-stitching both rectangles. This will have the character of a scarf, with a narrow hem of 0.5 cm (¼ in) backstitched on the machine.

1. Make a rectangle measuring 180 × 75 cm (71 × 29 ½ in), with D being the midpoint on the side marked A–B. From this point, measure 9 cm (3 ½ in) and mark point E. From this new point, measure 12 cm (4 ¾ in) perpendicularly for each side to obtain points F and F'. Complete the rectangle with points G and G', respectively 12 cm (4 ¾ in) from the previous points. This pattern is cut twice in crêpe material.

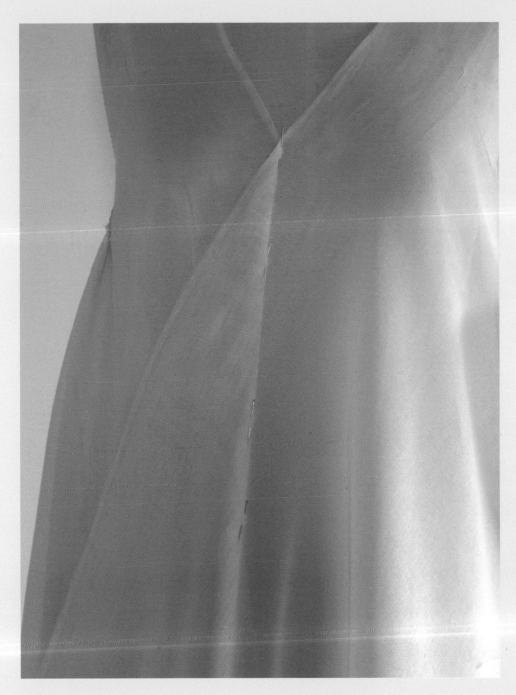

3. To assemble the dress, place the two rectangles on the mannequin, matching the D–E line with the shoulder and the space with the armhole. Join the two pieces at the front and back, decide upon the depth of the neckline and mark with a pin. From this point down to the bottom sew the pieces together front and back, but without exerting too much pressure since they are cut on the bias.

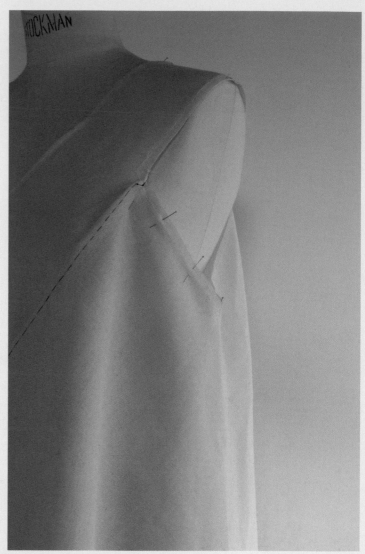

4. Next, pin the armholes together until you have the desired width, as shown in the photo.

5. The surplus fabric in the armhole is eased towards the front on the left side and the back on the right, then sewn to the armhole so as to evenly distribute the volume in the dress.

A view of the front of the dress, after assembly.

The back of the assembled dress.

Sheath dress

What stands out most in this fitted garment, designed by Leyre Valiente, is the overlaying of different pattern pieces. So as to distinguish one from the other, it is a good idea to use fabrics with different textures. Another striking feature is the ruffle sleeves, which, to make things easier, have been made using already-pleated satin, available on the market in a wide variety of colours and sizes.

This is a dress with lots of pieces, so you will need to be very careful when choosing fabrics and beads. It is important to give all the features a certain prominence, although care should be taken not to overload the garment.

Single-seam dress with a whorl of decorative ribbons

This is a semi-fitted garment, with a single seam down the back (where the zip is located). Its main focus is provided by the organza ribbons, and thus the fabric for the dress has been chosen to set these off: smooth to the touch, with clean draping qualities, silk provides the perfect canvas for this work of art.

The ribbons define the character of this dress, so choose colours that accord with the personality of the person wearing it, either warm or cool, or perhaps various shades of the same colour.

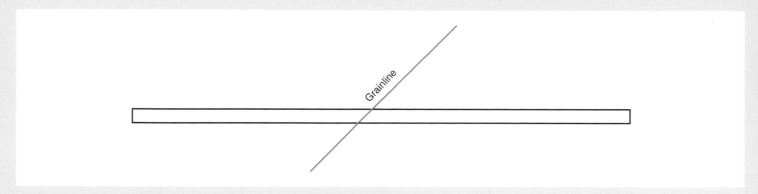

4. For the ribbons, cut out on the bias several rectangles of organza in various different colours, each measuring 30 × 1 cm (11 ¾ × ³/₈ in). In this case, I chose a warm colour palette made up of red, orange, ochre and brown.

5. To form the whorls adorning the hem and neckline, ribbons need to be attached one by one in uneven circles. This is done by sticking a 1 × 1 cm (³/₈ × ³/₈ in) square of Vilene® between the ribbon and the dress, and fusing it in place with a hot iron.

Tulle ruffle dress with single seam

This dress, with its flared shape, has been chosen for this book because it is so easy to make, and so flexible, making it a perfect example of the little black dress. A fairly lightweight fabric has been used to make this garment, since the tulle is what gives it body.

Due to the simplicity of the pattern for this dress, despite the tulle flounce it can be made with a textured fabric without being overwhelming. As a variation, a plain fabric can be used with coloured tulle.

Double layer dress with single seam

The uniqueness of this straight dress lies in the fact that, since it is folded over at the bottom, the hem does not need stiching. If this area were not specifically highlighted, it would probably not be so noticeable. However, since the intention was to do just that, extra volume was inserted when folding the fabric.

The simplicity of this dress makes it a perfect example of the little black dress, a basic item suitable for both day and evening wear, depending on the accessories (such as necklaces, bags or shoes) that are chosen to accompany it.

5. Since this is a dress made from a single pattern piece with a single seam, it is very easy to assemble. First, place the pattern on the mannequin and check the shoulder seams.

6. Then fold the pattern in half – joining the ends together for the neckline, shoulders and armholes – and sew at the back. To give the dress volume at the bottom, insert some small strips of tulle, 20 cm (7 7/8 in) in width, inside the garment.

Dress with Japanese sleeves

The bodice of this dress by Miguel Madriz should only be made from stretch tulle, a fabric known for its flexibility, to ensure that it fits correctly. From the different types available, I have used one with appliquéd, embossed motifs, such as can be purchased in any specialist fabric shop.

In addition to its volume, this dress also plays with transparency, both in the bodice with its patterned stretch tulle and in the skirt formed by layers of tulle, which billow out unevenly, creating more transparency in some areas than others.

Pleated dress

This dress is simple to make, since it only has one seam; however, the pleating might be a bit complicated. To make sure this process is successful, it is important to realise that the material should contain at least 20% synthetic fibre – it cannot be 100% natural fibre – if you want the pleats to remain in the garment. Further details are given in the glossary.

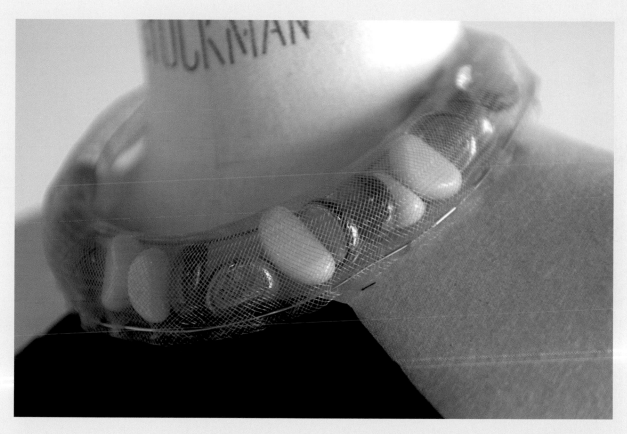

The collar on the dress was originally made of material, but the example shown in the photographs is a new variation, being replaced by a necklace of stones and material which can be stitched to the dress.

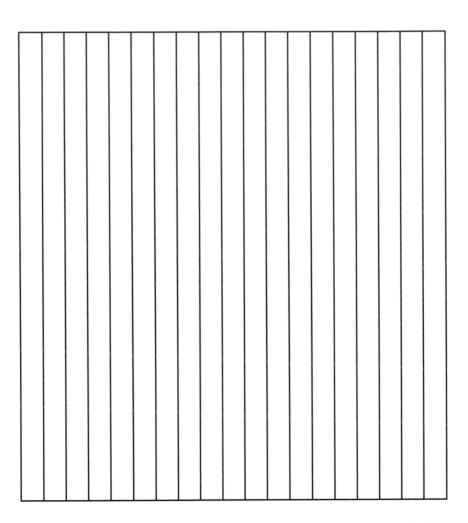

1. You need to pleat 285 cm (3 yds 4 in) of taffeta. So, before starting, a sufficient number of panels must be joined together to obtain this width, and the seams need to be pressed. The material is then hemmed and finally 19 panels are made, each measuring 5 cm (the final width of the pleated fabric will be 95 cm).

2. The panels should be pressed with an iron to ensure that they are clearly defined in the fabric, as shown in the picture. It is important to remember that the ideal temperature for ironing taffeta is between 100 °C (212 °F) and 160 °C (320 °F).

Asymmetric hem dress

The bodice of this dress is based on the famous dress worn by Audrey Hepburn in *Breakfast at Tiffany's*, which was voted the best dress in movie history. On the other hand, the skirt – whose distinctive draping falls from a circle cut out of a square – is much more contemporary. The two pieces combined result in a really chic little number.

The dress is cut with a high waistline. The bodice is fitted thanks to the two darts seen in the photograph, taking the form of a cross: one made down the centre front and the other across the centre of the bust.

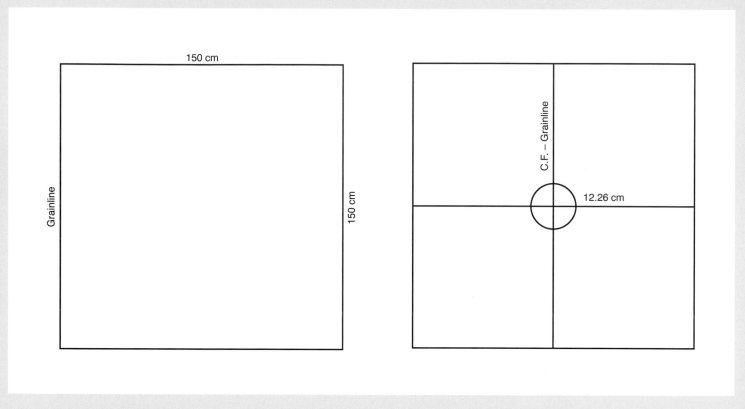

1. To begin making the pattern for this asymmetric dress, draw a square with sides measuring 150 cm (59 in).

2. Mark the midpoints on each side and join these up with two perpendicular lines. At the intersection of these lines (the centre of the square), draw a circle with a radius of 12.26 cm (4¹³/₁₆ in). This pattern is cut once in velvet.

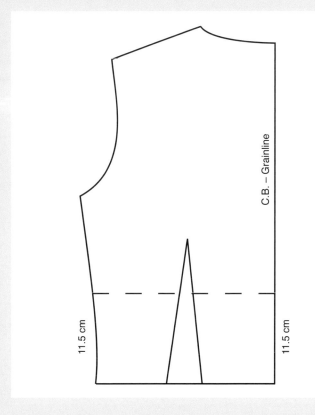

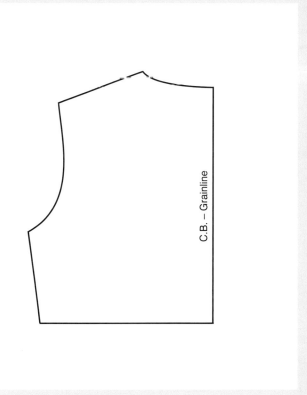

3. Next, take a basic pattern for a back piece and raise the waist by cutting across in a straight line 11.5 cm (4 ½ in) up from the bottom of the pattern.

4. Cut the pattern along the newly drawn line, ignoring the dart that was there.

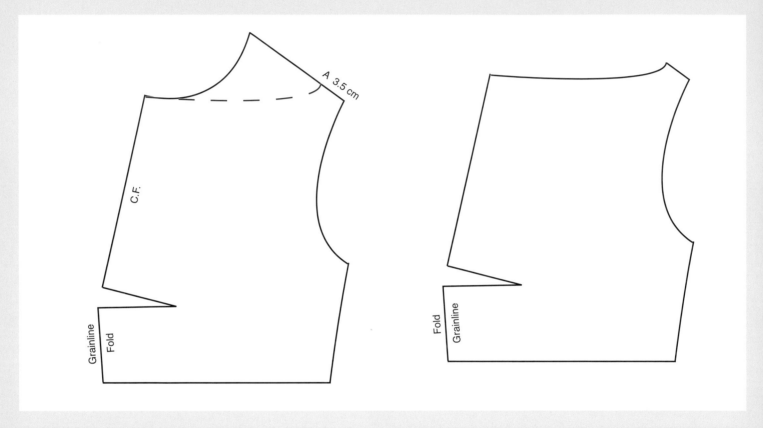

9. Adjust the width of the shoulder to 3.5 cm (1 3/8 in). To do this, draw a straight line from A to the corner of the centre front, with a slight curve at the shoulder to define the neckline.

10. The centre pattern piece should be cut 'on the fold', once in velvet and once in the fabric for the lining.

11. When assembling the pattern pieces, first of all place the centre pieces and the back in position and join, closing the darts, as shown in the picture. Then sew the skirt to the bodice.

High-waisted dress

This dress has a tight-fitting bodice and is tailored at the waist. Its voluminous skirt, with its mix of colours and textures, is made from three circles in different fabrics – plain taffeta, printed taffeta and printed silk organza – and a quarter circle in sinamay; this, being thicker than the other three fabrics, is rigid enough to support them.

The straps on the dress, which are a pair of chains, have beads on them for that special touch. Both chains come together at the neckline with a single stone, mimicking a necklace, while at the back there is a stone on each strap.

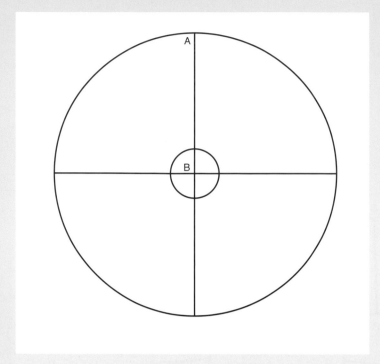

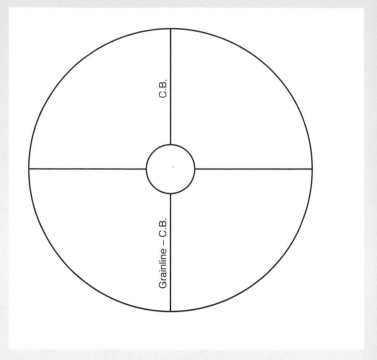

4. To make the pieces for the skirt draw one circle with a radius of 75 cm (29 ½ in) (the distance A–B) and another inner circle with a radius of 13.3 cm (5 ¼ in), both with the same centre.

5. Cut this pattern piece once in black taffeta, once in black striped taffeta, and once in checked silk organza.

6. To obtain the last pattern piece you need for this dress, extend the vertical diameter of the circle 30 cm (11¾ in) from E and mark point F, which is joined with a curve to C and D. Cut this piece once in black sinamay.

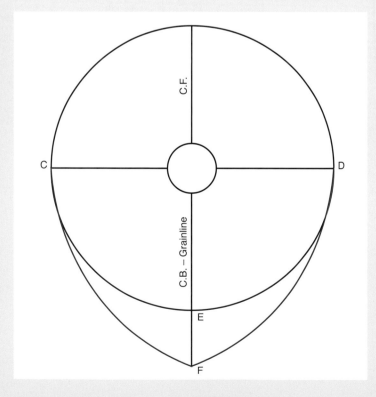

7. Place the bodice of the dress on the mannequin, joined at the back, and mark the folds in the neckline and waist with pins. Then sew the three circles to the bodice, gathering each edge to fit it to the contours of the body.

8. With the pieces joined together, even out the folds in the bust until they are perfect, as they are a fundamental feature of the silhouette and the waistline of the dress. When this is done, place the elongated sinamay circle with the tip pointing towards the back, which is gathered up to point N on the bodice. To finish, starting at the neckline (point B) sew in two thin chains, as far as point N, which will serve as the straps of the dress.

Dress with tuxedo neckline

This type of collar is typical of a formal dress, so for this reason I have chosen velvet and lace. Beneath the lace, I have used a golden fabric that highlights the motifs. If you prefer something a little more discreet, you can use a black fabric so that only one texture is perceived. If, on the other hand, you want something a bit bolder, you can use bright colours like fuchsia or lime green.

To close the dress, use a concealed zip, the advantage of which is that when closed it just looks like another seam. This can be placed on the centre back or on the lefthand side, whichever is more convenient.

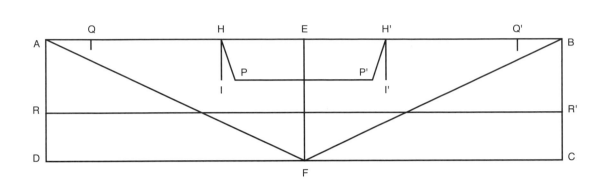

5. For the front, draw rectangle A-B-C-D measuring 114 × 27 cm (44⁷/₈ × 10⁵/₈ in) and then draw a line E–F dividing it in half. Mark H and H′ each at a distance of 18 cm (7 in) from E, and from these two new points draw a perpendicular line 9 cm (3½ in) long to obtain I and I′. 3 cm (1¹/₈ in) from each one,

mark points P and P′, which join up with H and H′, respectively. Points Q and Q′ should be marked 10 cm (4 in) from A and B and a notch made at each one. Finally, draw line R–R′ at a distance of 10.5 cm (4¹/₈ in) from C–D.

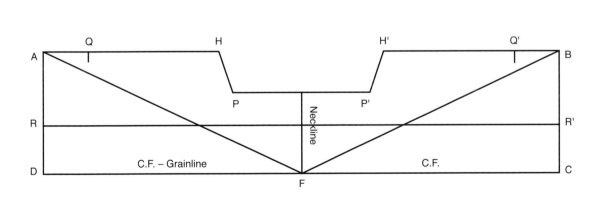

6. This pattern is cut once in velvet and once in the lining. The next step is to stitch wire into this piece along the lines Q–H, H′–Q′, C–D, P–P′, R–R′, A–F and F–B.

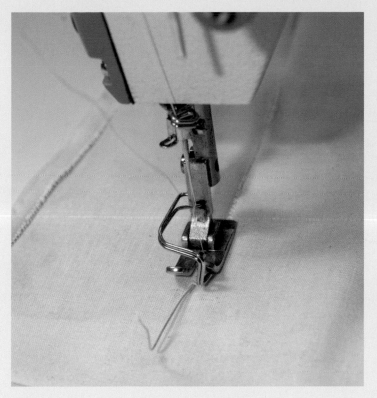

7. Wire (which should be thin and made of stainless steel so that it does not rust when the garment is washed) should be carefully stitched into the piece. This can either be done by hand or with a sewing machine, using a tiny zigzag stitch.

8. The pattern is assembled on the mannequin – making sure that Q–H and H′–Q′ match up with the armholes, H–P and P′–H′ with the shoulders and P–P′ with the collar – and joined to the back pieces of the pattern.

9. Shape the collar and the neckline by bending the wires until the desired volume and shape are achieved. Once the bodice is complete, sew the pieces for the skirt and overskirt.

Dress with sweetheart neckline

Strapless dresses like this one work better when made with stretch fabrics, since they fit the body more snugly and give the wearer more freedom of movement, making them feel more comfortable. For this design, Miguel Madriz, who created this dress, has chosen stretch satin, a fabric he combines with satin bows and a tulle overskirt.

The satin bows are features that have been incorporated to embellish the garment rather than for functional purposes, and therefore need to be highlighted: the colour of the one at the front is fuchsia, while the one at the back is much longer than the dress itself.

TOWER HAMLETS COLLEGE
POPLAR HIGH STREET
LONDON
E14 0AF

12. Finally, to make the overskirt, draw a rectangle measuring 100 × 200 cm (39³/₈ × 78³/₄ in) and cut twice in black tulle.

13. To assemble the dress, first of all place the four pieces (front and back pieces for bodice and skirt) on the mannequin and join them together. Then sew the flounce at the same height as the skirt.

14. Finally, as shown in the photograph, gather up the flounce a little to give it body and assemble the tulle rectangles in two layers, so that they billow out over the skirt. To finish, place the fuchsia bow on the bust and the black bow on the back.

Dress with camellia skirt

This is a classic, elegant dress, with a shape that evokes Christian Dior's New Look of the glamorous 1950s. The dress is tailored at the waist and hugs the body, with darts at the armholes. This contrasts with the fullness of the skirt, achieved thanks to the three circles that give it shape. To accentuate the shape, a rigid, lightweight fabric has been chosen.

The camellia – the flower with those huge, well-defined petals – embellishes the hemline of this dress. Although normally used in wedding dresses, this example shows that the camellia is the perfect adornment for a simple cocktail dress.

6. When assembling the dress, place the front and back pieces of the pattern on the mannequin, and close and sew up the darts in the bust.

7. Next sew the skirt to the bodice. To do this, sew the semi-circles one by one to the front or back of the dress, and to each other, as shown in the picture.

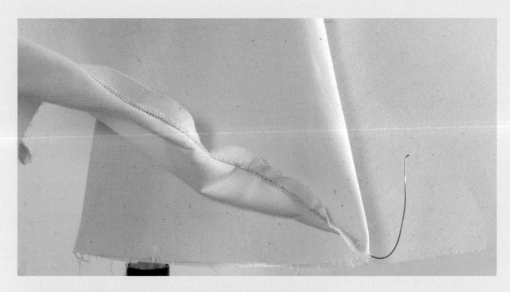

8. Stitch a wire – made of stainless steel and of average thickness (the thickness will depend on the weight of the material) that is easy to manipulate – 2 cm (¾ in) from the edge all the way around the hem of the skirt using a zigzag stitch. Then fold over, to give the dress volume and simulate the shapes of camellias.

Patterns drawn to scale

The patterns for all the dresses featured throughout the book are shown here drawn to scale, along with the basic patterns needed to make them. It is important to remember to leave an allowance for the seams and hems when tracing them out on the fabric.

Basic pattern

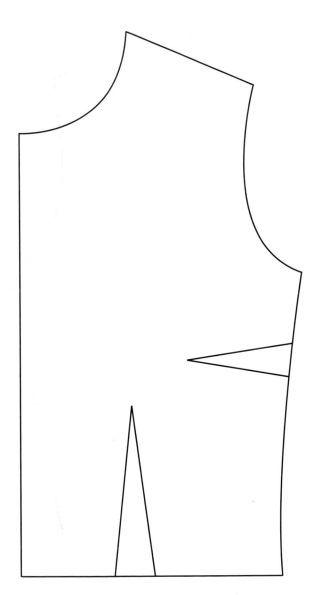

Basic pattern for front piece on scale of 1:3

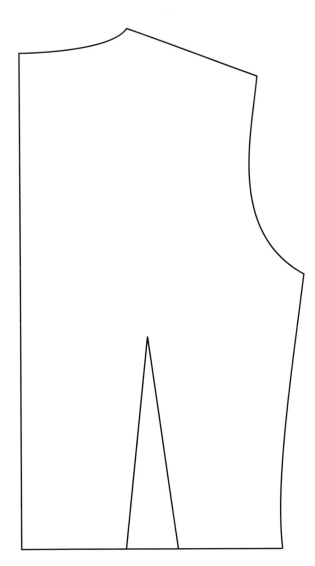

Basic pattern for back piece on scale of 1:3

Straight basic pattern piece

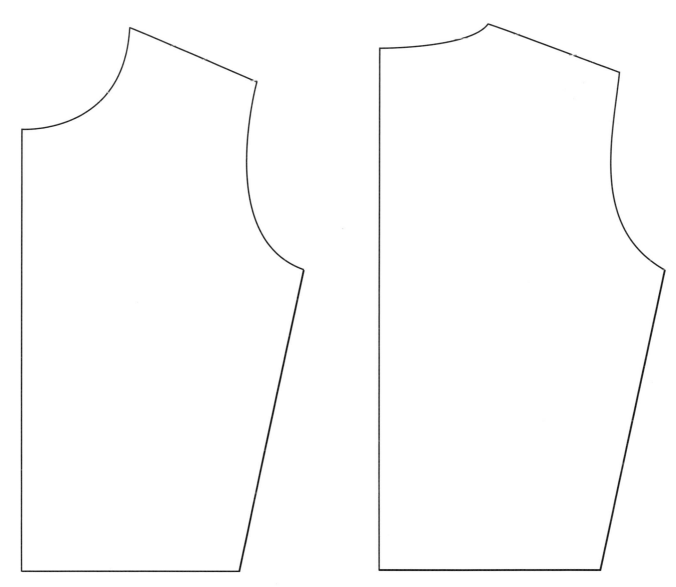

Basic pattern for front piece on scale of 1:3

Basic pattern for back piece on scale of 1:3

Long basic pattern piece

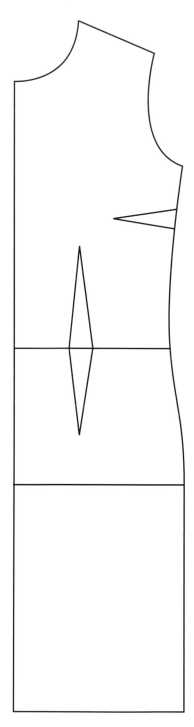

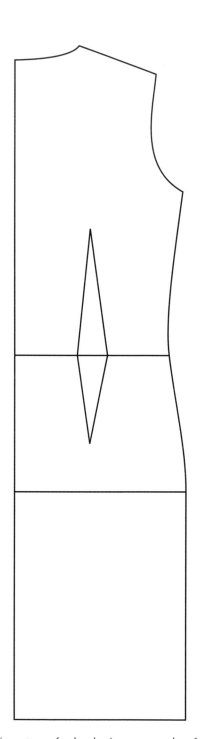

Basic pattern for front piece on scale of 1:5

Basic pattern for back piece on scale of 1:5

Long, straight basic pattern piece

Basic pattern for front piece on scale of 1:5

Basic pattern for back piece on scale of 1:5

Trapezoid dress

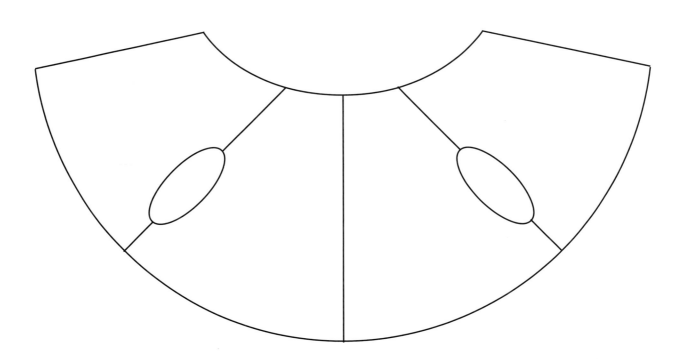

Pattern for top part of dress on scale of 1:5

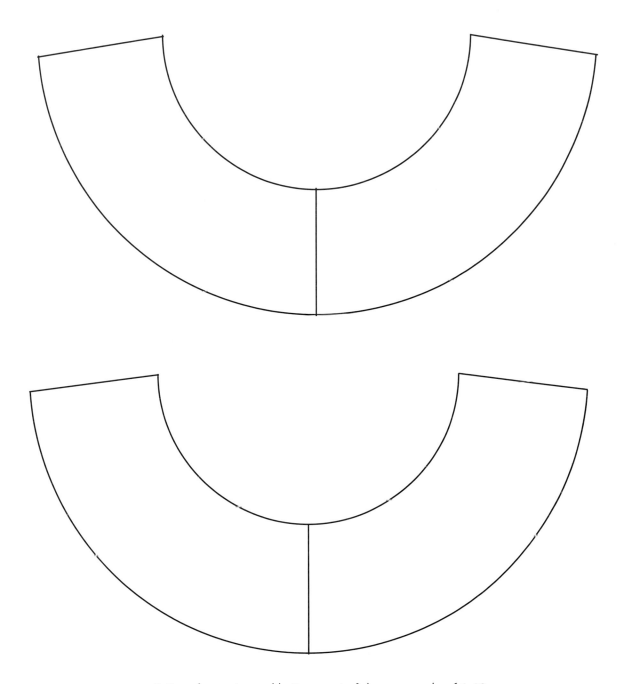

Pattern for centre and bottom part of dress on scale of 1:10

Halterneck dress

Pattern for dress and facing on scale of 1:10

Cocoon-shaped dress

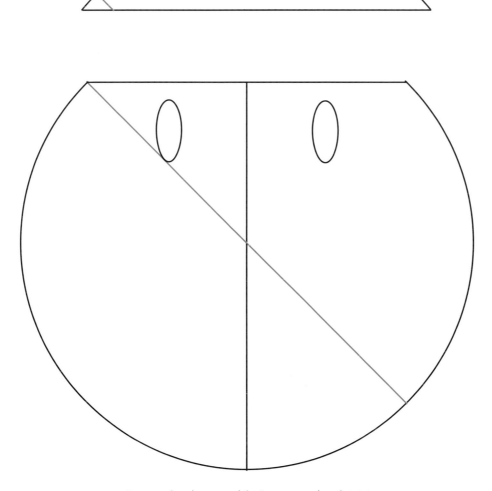

Pattern for dress and facing on scale of 1:10

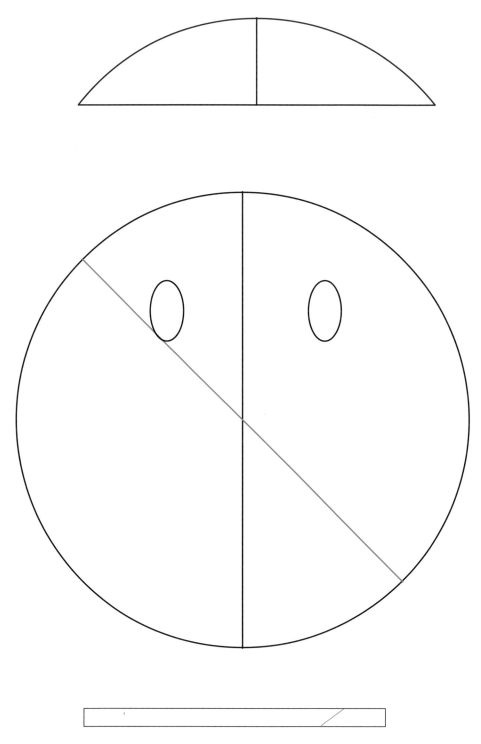

Pattern for overskirt, flounces and bows on scale of 1:10

Flexible dress

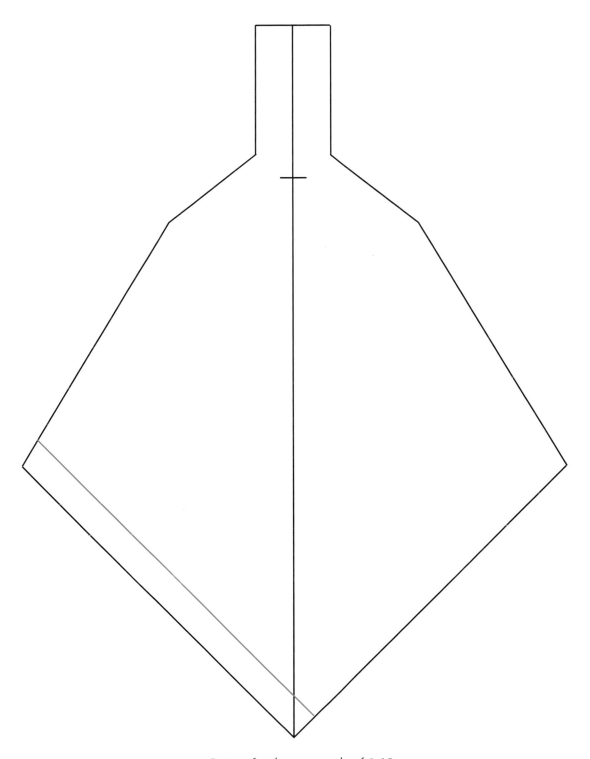

Pattern for dress on scale of 1:10

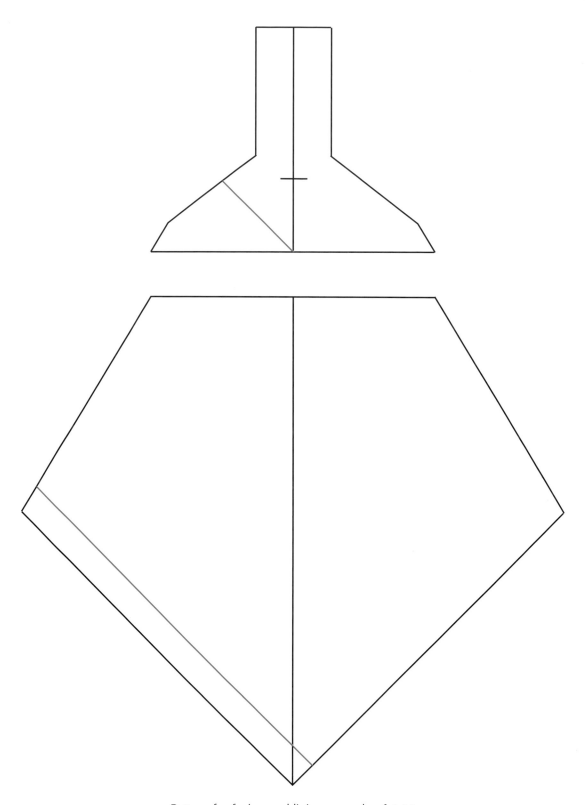

Pattern for facing and lining on scale of 1:10

Dress with draping scarves

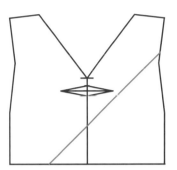

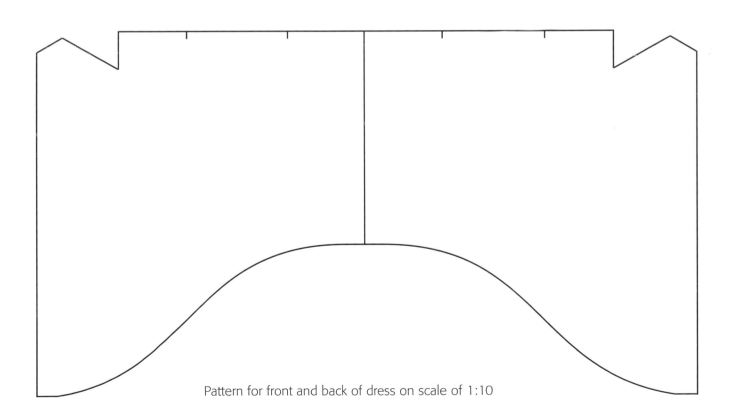

Pattern for front and back of dress on scale of 1:10

Dress with Japanese sleeves

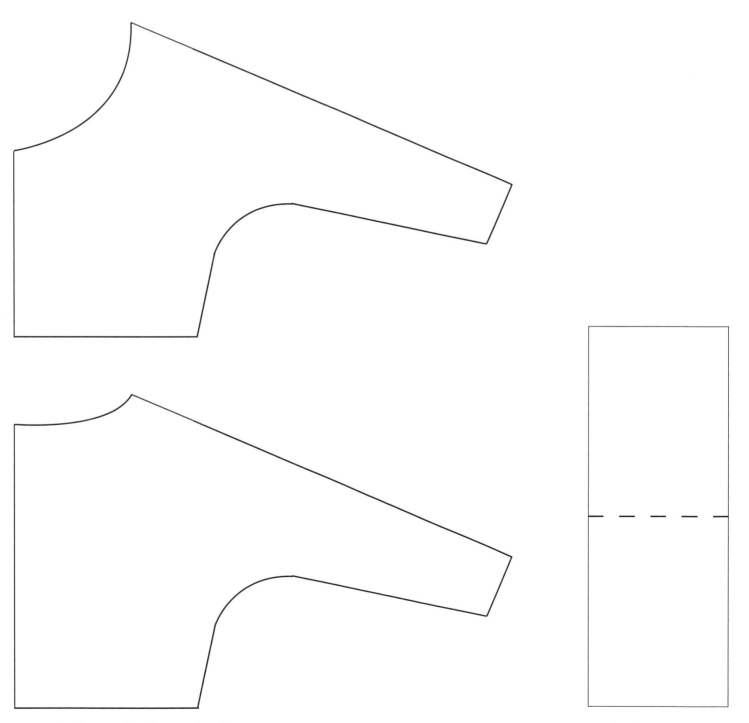

Pattern for front and back on scale of 1:4

Pattern for skirt on scale of 1:30

Pleated dress

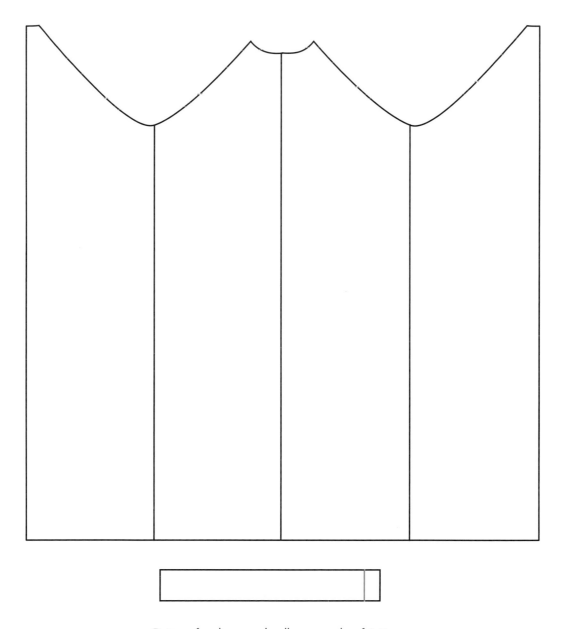

Pattern for dress and collar on scale of 1:7

Asymmetric hem dress

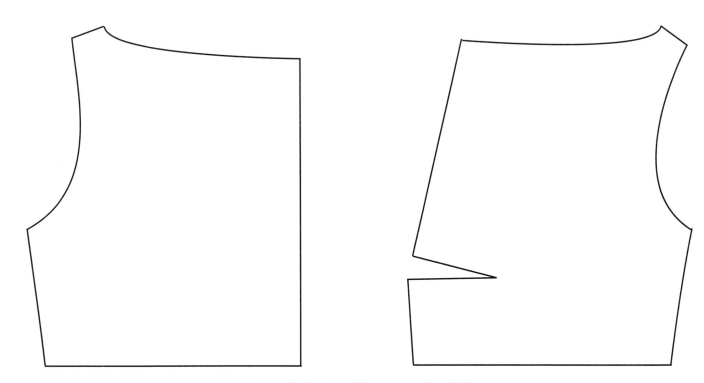

Pattern for back and front on scale of 1:3

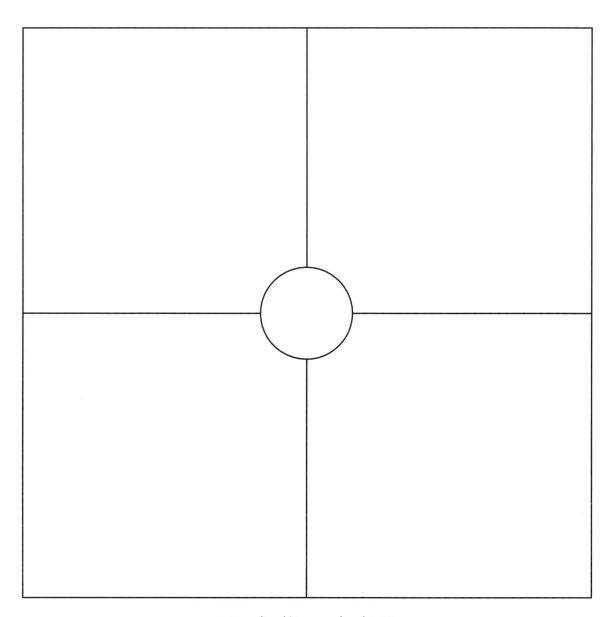

Pattern for skirt on scale of 1:10

High-waisted dress

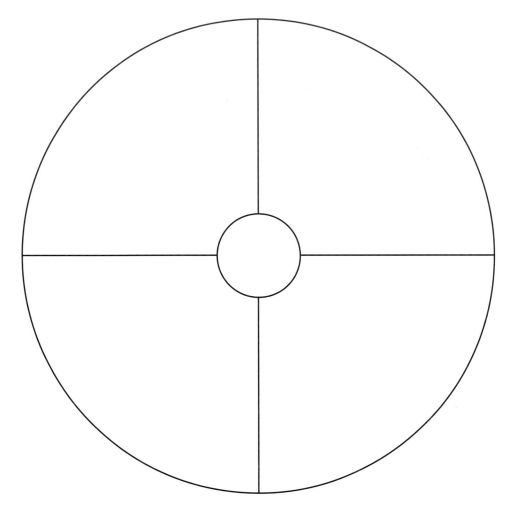

Pattern for skirt on scale of 1:12

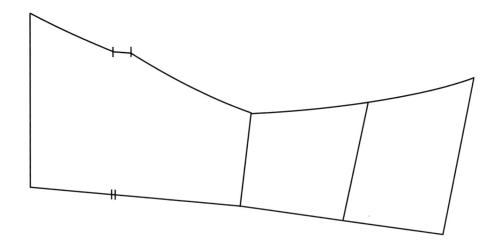

Pattern for bodice on scale of 1:4

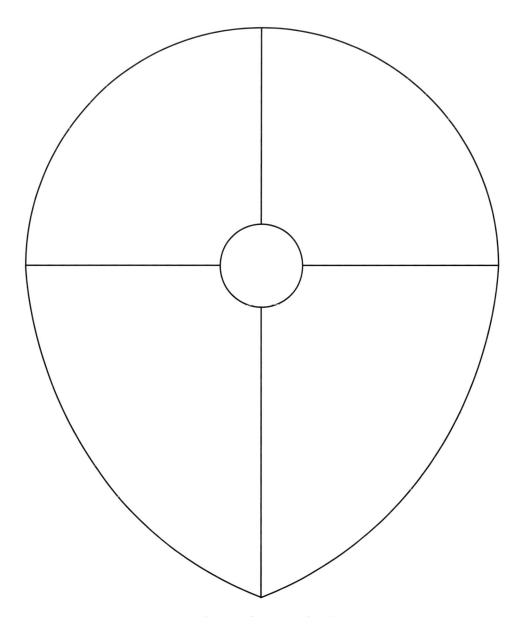

Pattern for overskirt on scale of 1:12

Dress with tuxedo neckline

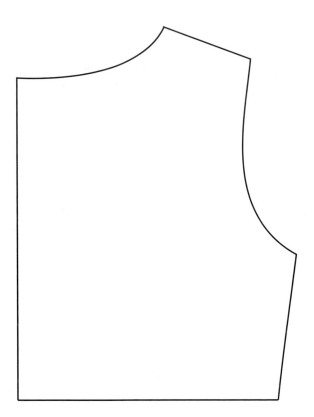

Pattern for back on scale of 1:3

Pattern for skirt on scale of 1:7

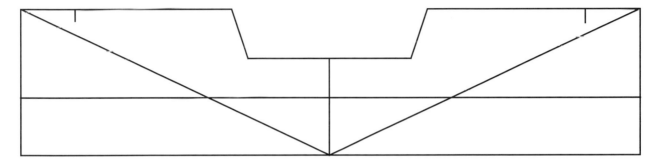

Pattern for front on scale of 1:7

Pattern for overskirt on scale 1:10

Dress with sweetheart neckline

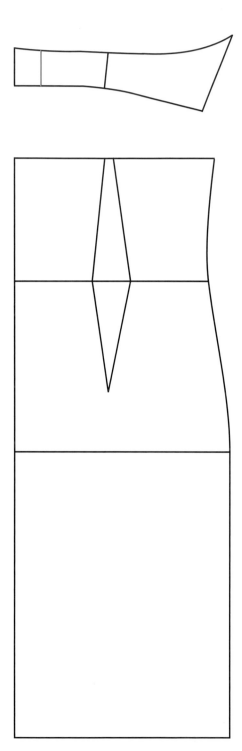

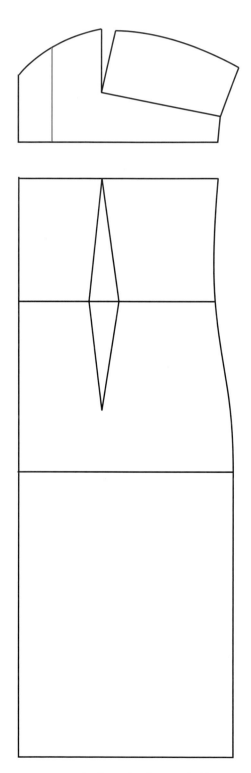

Pattern for back bodice and skirt
on a scale of 1:4

Pattern for front bodice and skirt
on a scale of 1:4

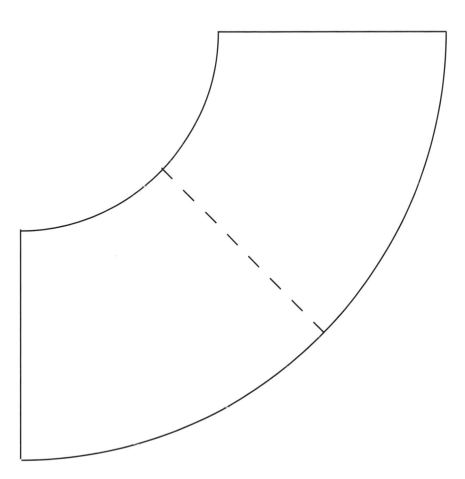

Pattern for flounce on a scale of 1:5

Pattern for front bow on scale of 1:2

Glossaries

Glossary of patternmaking and dressmaking terms

Against the grain: is the horizontal direction of a fabric, corresponding to the weave.

Bias: in a square of fabric, the bias is the diagonal line that divides the square into two identical halves. Fabrics cut on the bias, i.e. diagonal with regard to the direction of the thread, provide garments with movement.

Bust dart: is the dart that creates the volume of the bust.

Casing: a crease that is made on a garment leaving a space through which a ribbon, rubber band or cord is passed.

Centre back (C.B.): is the imaginary line that divides the back in half, lengthwise. In a pattern, the C.B. is the line that indicates the centre back of the body.

Centre front (C.F.): is the imaginary line that divides the body in half, lengthwise, at the front. In a pattern, the C.F. is the line that indicates the centre front of the body.

Cocoon-shaped silhouette: is when the garments are very voluminous and puffed out. Inspired by caterpillar cocoons, Paul Poiret (1879--1944) was the first designer to use this design idea, in the second decade of the last century. Since then, it has become a staple on the runways of many designers around the world.

Crease: a fold in the fabric to adjust the garment (as in the use of darts) or to give it fullness (as in the use of pleats).

Dart: is a fold made in the fabric, its volume adjusted to alter fit of the garment.

Drape: a basic characteristic of every fabric, determined by the way the fabric was manufactured and the weight of the fibre. Natural fibres have the best draping qualities.

Évasé: describes the A-line silhouette of a garment.

Facing: a fabric that is used to finish the borders of garments. As long as the garment has facings, they are cut both in the fabric and the interfacing of the seams following the same direction as the thread and the fabric. The interfacing is stuck with the heat of the iron, not with steam.

Flounce: generally, a rectangular piece of fabric (although it may have a circular or spiral form) which is puckered to create a fullness at the hemline, cuffs, collars, etc.

Fullness: width or extension of a garment in the part that does not hug the body.

Grainline (in a pattern): the grainline corresponds to the direction of the warp of the fabric and indicates the direction in which to place the fabric when cutting it.

Hem: a piece of fabric folded and sewn at the bottom of a garment to give it a neat finish. It involves leaving a greater margin of fabric when cutting the pattern than the total length of the garment, to take account of the hem.

Hook: a metal clasp consisting of two parts, one shaped as a handle that clasps, the other in the shape of a latch. Used to hold together two parts of a garment.

Interfacing: fabric that is placed between the fabric of the garment and the facing or lining, with the aim of strengthening it.

Invisible zip: a zip that when closed cannot be seen and looks like any other seam, helping the garment to achieve a clean aesthetic. For this reason dresses featured in this book use this type of zip. They are sewn using a special foot that is attached to the machine and can be purchased at any shop where you can also buy zips.

Lining: fabric lining the inside of a garment. Primarily it is used to give the garment a cleaner finish, so that the reverse is aesthetically pleasing. The pattern specifies which parts correspond to the lining of a garment. In the case of dresses, the pieces are usually the same size, but in coats, the pieces are larger.

Loop: a piece that can take various forms (usually metal or plastic), with one or more central hinges that serve to adjust straps or belts.

Mannequin: a representation of the human body, used for the assembly, fitting and display of clothes.

Mock-up: or *toile:* the first made-up version of a garment. It is generally created in a white or natural colour, and if the garment is symmetrical, only half of it is made.

Neckline: an opening in a garment formed by the line of the neck and part of the chest or back. It also refers to the bust area that is left exposed in a garment.

Notch: a small cut made on the edge of the pattern, used as a guide or reference point for its correct assembly.

On the fold: when the pattern must be placed along the folded edge of the fabric before cutting.

Opening: a slash in a garment to facilitate its movement or for aesthetic purposes.

Pleats: permanent creases that are made in the fabric, usually though the application of heat. Three times more fabric is required than the width of the final garment, with sometimes up to three panels of fabric having to be joined to achieve the maximum width, depending on the width of the chosen fabric.

Pompom: a group of threads or cords that are joined together at one end and hang loose at the other end, like a decoration in the shape of a ball or half a ball.

Pucker: to reduce or gather a fabric to a certain measurement using threads which are pulled to achieve the effect.

Puff out: to embellish fabric with wide creases.

Right-angled triangle: a triangle with one angle measuring 90°.

Ruffling: refers to small folds, made outwards or inwards, in the fabric.

Seam: a series of stitches joining two pieces of a garment together.

Square: to draw, from one point, a line at a right angle to an existing line.

Take in: to eliminate excess fabric so that the garment is smoother and lighter.

Toile: see Mock-up.

Vilene®: a very fine interlining that is used to stick together delicate fabrics such as silk. This is done using an iron.

Waistband: a strap or belt with a buckle or clasp to fasten certain items of clothing at the waist.

Waist dart: is the dart made on the curve of the waist of a garment.

Fabrics

Acetate: a synthetic fibre made from cellulose, it can be mixed with cotton or silk. It is a soft fibre that drapes well.

Cambric: a fine closely-woven fabric made from thread or cotton.

Cheesecloth: generally cotton fabric. Its characteristic lengthwise ruffles or creases give it a certain level of elasticity.

Cool wool: is very fine and lightweight sheep's hair. These characteristics make it perfect as a summer fabric.

Crêpe: also known as crape, this fabric has a granulated and ruffled surface with light elasticity.

Georgette: is a lightweight, fine and somewhat wrinkled fabric. It is made from silk, but can also be synthetic. Its name comes from the 20th century Parisian fashion designer Madame Georgette de la Plante.

Knitwear: using cotton, wool, silk or synthetic fibres, it is handmade with needles, crochet hooks or on a machine. It is characterized by its flexibility, elasticity and the ease with which it adapts to the body.

Lace: a handmade ornamental and semi-transparent fabric decorated with embroidery.

Organza: a transparent silk or cotton fabric. Crisp to the touch, it creases and shapes like paper.

Ottoman: corded-effect fabric, often made of silk. It is used both in dressmaking and in tapestry.

***Paillette* fabric:** a fabric with sequins.

Raw silk: also called *bourette*, this is a grainy, matt fabric. Heavier than common silk, it has a rustic, dull appearance.

Rayon: also known as viscose, it is made from wood or cotton fibres, resulting in a smooth, light, cool fabric.

Satin: silk or cotton, characterized by its glossiness and smoothness.

Sinamay: a fabric obtained from manila or pita fibre. Its appearance is similar to raffia.

Taffeta: a closely woven silk fabric, it does not have a right and a wrong side. Sometimes it can have a 'shot' effect.

Tulle: a fine, transparent and light-mesh fabric, often made of silk, cotton or synthetic fibre.

Velvet: in silk, cotton or acetate, this fabric has a distinctive short pile. It should be cut with the hair facing upwards, as this makes the colour more intense, but usually it is cut in the opposite direction with the result that once the garment is completed the colours lose their brightness. When it is sewn, never iron it forcefully (as this will crush the hair and change the colour); instead, gently press the iron on the garment.

Viscose: see **Rayon.**

Acknowledgements

To Carlos Bandrés, to whom I am forever in debt for his dedication, patience and expertise.

To my mother and my sister: my inspiration.

To my family and friends, for their encouragement and for believing in me.

To the Istituto Europeo di Design and the headquarters of the Palacio de Altamira in Madrid, for providing the best possible backdrop for the photos.

And special thanks to my niece, Isabel, for her understanding and endless love, in spite of all the time that I missed out on being with her.